GOOGLE CLASSROOM 2020

A complete User Manual to learn all there is to using Google classroom effectively

BY

MARVIS KEN

Contents

WHAT IS GOOGLE CLASSROOM

Google Classroom is a tool that teachers can use to create, collect, and grade assignments. It is a cross-platform tool that can be used on almost any device connected to the Internet. There are mobile apps for iOS and Android, as well as a website, and everything is synced across all devices so you can manage your class anywhere.

WHAT DOES GOOGLE CLASSROOM DO

Google Classroom is constantly updated with new features and functions. As of today, you will find a shortlist of the functions that were taken from the product description of the app in the App Store:

- The classroom is designed to help teachers create, collect, and evaluate paperless assignments. This includes time-saving features such as the ability to automatically create a copy of a Google document for each student.

- Drive folders are also created for each task and student so that everyone stays organized.
- The simple homework workflow enables teachers to quickly create, review, and grade assignments in one place.
- Students can view all of their assignments on a homework page, and all teaching materials (e.g. documents, photos, and videos) are automatically stored in folders on Google Drive

REASONS WHY WE SHOULD USE GOOGLE CLASSROOM

If you've used Google Classroom in the past few years, you're probably already "sold" because using it is a good thing. But if it's new to you, you probably want to know why this change is good for students. Here are a few things to consider:

1. Google Classroom is easy to use. Compared to other LMSs (Learning Management Systems) that have been popular in the last decade, Google Classroom is incredibly simple. Establishing a new class does not take much time or experience. Our technology team was trained for about an hour, and by the end of the session, we had all established a classroom.

2. Google Classroom can help you communicate more efficiently. You only enter the students' email addresses once and communication takes place in the classroom. Simply by entering the student in the classroom, an email group, a discussion group, and a Google

Calendar for the teacher are automatically created. And it's easy to add and remove students from the class as needed.

3. You can communicate more effectively with Google Classroom. Probably more important than easy to use and efficient, communication tools are also very effective. Since everything is cloud-based, student assignments are no longer lost. When a student is absent, communication is perfect. Last month, Google Classroom added a parent notification feature to keep parents up-to-date on what's happening in the "classroom."

4. Google Classroom is cheaper and greener. I'm not completely excited about paperless learning, especially for younger students. However, I see a real advantage in that schools are cheaper to copy and print. If every student already has a device that connects to the Internet, each sheet of paper that we store will only make the school more efficient and environmentally friendly.

5. Therefore, students will continue to learn in the future ... so I will probably have to drop my "paperless" phone. Universities no longer expect students to print their five-page essays. As K-12 educators, we must take note of our students and prepare them for the world in which they will live.

6. It's best for struggling students ... as long as you help them manage the device. (The device itself can sometimes be a distraction, so the administration needs to be taught.)

7. The reason Google Classroom is better is because of the organizational advantage it offers them. Homework is never lost and each classroom is already organized by the teacher. However, navigation must be taught for these students. Although students are digital natives, it does not mean that they understand how adults organize their world to help them learn.

8. With Google Classroom, collaboration outside of school is easier (i.e. flipped classroom). Again, it is cloud-based and accessible from anywhere with a

connection. Students can share assignments and collaborate from home to complete them. Cooperation is not limited to working in a group with other colleagues. A teacher can change the classroom by sharing a video that is streamed live at night. Students should see it that afternoon to prepare for an exam the next day. The possibilities are endless.

9. Teacher planning is easy and the delivery time is worth it. New additional features in Google Classroom allow teachers to plan homework in the future. Certain assignments could be posted on a Monday in October and then closed on that Friday. If a teacher is away for a long time, they can plan assignments and don't have to rely on a substitute to manage everything. Classrooms can also be used from semester to semester and from year to year. It would be terrible for a teacher to copy and paste.

HOW TO MANAGE GOOGLE CLASSROOM

Management Techniques Decrease Font Size Increase Font Size Font Size Print Email How to Manage Your Classroom: Classroom Management Techniques Classroom management is a very important aspect of teaching. Once you have put together your classroom management strategies, you will discover that teaching is a pleasure and that your students perform well. This article is intended to give you some tips to help you with your class management strategies. Get ready. You should be prepared every time you enter your class. Children know when their teacher has done their homework and respect the fact that their teacher cares enough about their learning to prepare them for class. Every day, you should plan your day carefully by developing a daily schedule and lesson plan that is closely aligned with school district regulations. These plans generally must address the needs and learning styles of each student in their classroom. In other words, students who learn visually should receive lessons and activities that match their learning styles. Students who have auditory learners should receive instructions in this area. Students who need additional time should receive this time. High-level students should have extra time, homework assignments, etc. If you are prepared, you and your students will have a pleasant and productive day every day. Make your room attractive. You must work to have an attractive room that you and your students can appreciate and enjoy. This environment sets the tone of learning. So take time to make your room attractive and conducive to learning. Display attractive bulletin boards in your room that show things you and your students are doing, such as: For example, your student's work, art projects, science exhibits, or other notable information in the classroom. Your room may also have learning centers, a room library, a play area, a listening center, a computer, a science corner, etc. Get creative and make it an attractive place to study. Establish lesson rules.

• **Teaching rules**: Children must follow the rules, and you need guidelines that your children must follow to teach and make the most of the day. Sit down with your students at the beginning of the year or anytime to make rules for living in your room and other parts of the building. Research has shown that students who participate in setting up their rules are more likely to follow them. Therefore, let your students work with you on this project. Once these rules are established, it is everyone's responsibility to ensure that the rules are followed. You can set up some sort of short-term reward for those who follow the rules, e.g. Stickers, stars, pencils, or other signs for your students. Be enthusiastic about your lessons. When teaching a lesson, teach it as if you love what you do and interact with your students and get them involved. Develop a method of calling each of your students and don't let some of your talkative students dominate the class. Encourage all your students to participate in your classes. If a student gives an incorrect answer, encourage and help them succeed by helping them find the correct answer by giving clues, asking questions, and examining them. Be sure to always thank all students for participating in the class. Remember to give students enough time to answer the question, as all students are different and some take longer than others. You will never want to turn off your students so that the answers flow and keep getting the most out of them. Be fair to your students. As a teacher, you must be fair to all your students. Make sure students are always heard and treat each one with dignity and respect. Make no difference to them and respect both those who seem a little disobedient and those who respectfully present themselves all the time. Everyone will love and appreciate her for this attitude of being fair to all students. Keep good student records.

In addition to setting a due date for an assignment, instructors can set a specific date range within which students can submit the assignment. These dates are called availability dates. This data is optional and can be configured according to how you want to manage the allocation.

Exam availability dates may affect student shipments. For more information, see the Questionnaire Availability Dates lesson.

In the Due Date and Availability Date fields, Canvas displays the time zone date and time based on context. If you manage courses in a different time zone than your local time zone and create or edit a due date for a task, the course and local times are displayed for reference.

If multiple valuation periods are activated in a course, only expiration dates are valid for closed valuation periods. Availability dates do not apply.

The expiration date is the expiration date and time of the order. Student assignments submitted after the due date are marked late in the grade book. Due dates are not required in Canvas but are useful for managing course workflow and deadlines.

You can also set a specific time as the appropriate date part. If you change an expiration time for an assignment, the second's value is 0 by default, unless the minute's value is set to 59. In this case, the seconds are also set to 59. For example, if you set a due date on September 19 at 4: 3 pm, each student submission sent after September 19 at 4:15 pm will be marked late.

If time is not set, the default time is 23:59:59 for the course time zone, and homework is marked late at 12:00:00. For example, if you set an expiration date for September 19 at 11:59 p.m., the assignment will be marked late if it is submitted on or after September 20 at 12:00 am

If you want to create a date range in which students can view and submit an assignment, you can set availability dates. Availability dates can also be called blackout dates.

Available from [1]: Date and time when homework is available to students. If the time is not set, the default date for the course time zone is noon.

To [2]: Date and time when students can no longer submit the assignment. If time is not set, the default time for the course time zone is 11:59 p.m. and the task closes at noon the next day.

When the assignment is published, the fields in empty fields with availability dates can be submitted at any time during the course.

After saving the assignment, you can view the assignment details. If there is a due date for the assignment, the date is displayed under the Due Date [1] heading. If availability dates are available, they are displayed under the Available from and to titles [2].

You can also view the details of all tasks on the task index page.

On tests, to date does not restrict student's access to display their test result. For example, you may not want students to show their test results to date. To make this change, you must edit the test options and limit the test results.

If you want to keep an assignment open throughout the course, don't set availability dates. If no availability dates are set, all users can submit the assignment at the end of the course.

ADD STUDENT TO A CLASS IN GOOGLE CLASSROOM

After setting up a class in Google Classroom, you want to invite students to take the class. You can invite as many students as you want. You can invite the students in your class or give them a code they can use to sign up for your class (which is the easiest way!).

You can invite students from the school directory or your contacts or group lists. Just follow these steps:

In the Select Students to Invite dialog box, select the checkboxes next to all the students you want to invite to the class.

Click Invite Student.

Your class list will be updated to include the students you just invited. Guest students will receive an email asking them to attend the class. Each student must click on the link in the email to attend the class.

Students must have an email address that belongs to the school domain, p. B. myname@myuniversity.edu. You cannot invite anyone outside your school domain.

If you have a large number of students to choose from, use the search box above to find the students in your class.

Invite students with the access code.

To save time by inviting all of your students, you can let your students take responsibility for inviting you to class with a special access code. That's how:

Log in to your class and receive the class code at the bottom left.

Give this code to your students in the most convenient way (for example, writing it on your class board or including it in a brochure).

Tell students to go to classes.google.com, click the plus sign at the top, and enter the code to attend the class.

If for any reason you need to disable or reset the postcode, go to the Stream tab for your class and click on the drop-down menu next to the pass code. Reset assigns a new code to the class, which disables the old code. Students must join the class using the new code. If you disable this code, students will no longer be able to access the class with this code.

HOW TO RATE ASSIGNMENT IN GOOGLE CLASSROOM

With Google Classroom, the times when students submitted papers and assignments are over. As a teacher, you can do your homework in class with additional materials such as brochures or worksheets. Students complete the task and send it back electronically via Google Drive. After your students return to their assignments, you can even grade them online. That's how it goes:

- Log in to your class and click the Stream tab if it isn't already displayed. You can see the tasks you have performed in the middle column.
- In the Task field, you can see how many students have completed the task and have not completed it. Click the number above done. You will see the list of students who submitted the task.

- Click on the student's name to expand their task
- To see what the student submitted, click on the document attached to the student's task. The document is opened in the corresponding Google application (e.g. Google Docs).
- Make any comments you have in the document.
- You can design your comments differently to stand out from the student text. Just like before, when teachers used red pens to mark a task, you can add comments with red text. Or, even better, you can use the comment tool to post comments. Simply select the text you are commenting on and choose Insert → Comment. Write your comment and click the comment. All of your comments are automatically saved in the document submitted by the student.
- Close the document to return to the student's work page.
- To rate the task; click where it says "No rating".

- Enter the number of points between 0 and 100. No letters are accepted in this field.
- Check the box next to the student's task.
- Click back. Homework must be returned to students before being recorded.
- The classroom asks you if you want to return the task and if you want to give feedback. When you're done, click Return Assignment.
- The assignment is displayed as returned in the task list. The student receives an email that sends the task back and can edit and send it back if necessary.
- When creating worksheets for tasks, it's best to use Google Drive applications like Google Docs, Spreadsheets, etc. This is because Google Apps are fully integrated with the Classroom. If you use third-party applications such as Microsoft Word, you and your students will need to download, reload, and reconnect the files to the task. Using Google Apps eliminates extra work.

●

HOW TO KEEP YOUR STUDENT MOTIVATED

How do you keep the students motivated? I like to compare it to maintaining a healthy and successful marriage. As with passion, motivation wanes if you don't feed it every day. It takes time, effort, and energy, but it's worth it.

In my experience, a motivated teacher motivates the students. If you are passionate about teaching, your students are more likely to show a passion for learning. However, I'm afraid that it works the other way round too: if you don't mind teaching, your students won't mind learning.

You won't motivate your students if you don't involve them and let them play an active role in your classes. Gone are the days when the teachers spoke most of the class and the students played a passive role? Classes must be student-centered. The teacher must act as a coach and moderator. to support, guide, and guide the learning process.

Allow the students to shine

It is also important to give students a chance to succeed. Give them tasks so that they can see the results of their efforts

Make your lessons unforgettable. Use games and competitions. They all love competitions and it gives students a good opportunity to interact, have fun, and learn at the same time.

Bring authentic materials that your students can connect to and that meet their needs and interests. Create your activities and show them that you are willing to put a lot of effort and time into making them successful.

Explain why you are doing certain things

There is nothing more boring than a teacher telling students to open their book on page 22 and ask them to do exercise five. You should explain why this exercise is important to you and what you can achieve with it.

Give very clear instructions.

Be clear when setting up a task and give students time to prepare and ask questions first. There is nothing more frustrating for them than not being able to work well because they have not understood the task. This is very important for students. You have to have a very clear idea of what to do.

You want your students to leave your class and think it was worth it. Start your lesson by writing your lesson plan in the corner of the board so students know what they will learn. At the end of the lesson, show the schedule and review everything you've learned. They must see where they are now and where they will lead next.

Students are required to work in pairs or groups. Get them out of their seats and move. Ask them to change partners regularly. To get your students' attention, set up a variety of meaningful and interesting activities, and create a friendly atmosphere in which they feel they can speak freely and ask questions.

We all know that our students prefer to look at a screen than at a book. So use pictures, flashcards, infographics, quizzes, and new technologies. Many websites offer online quizzes, games, or videos

BEST CHROME EXTENSION FOR TEACHER

Google Chrome is increasingly where it is.

Google Chrome becomes the de facto Internet browser and delivers Internet Explorer for the first time after a five-year free fall of Microsoft's unfavorable software. Now quickly start the counter and draw darker images for the Google Chrome competition with Safari, Firefox, and IE still below Chrome's market share of nearly 50%.

The real story is more complicated, as Microsoft combines IE with Windows to create a large integrated user base, the rise of Google Chrome books, Apple's elegant Safari, which is only for iOS, and a subtle change from the mobile browser to the applications. That further spoils the image. What is the best or most popular browser is not easy.

But for the here and now with regards to browsers, Google Chrome is king, and part of what makes it great is Google Chrome

WHAT ARE GOOGLE CHROME EXTENTION

Extensions are "applications that run in the Chrome browser and additional features that offer integration with third-party websites or services and personalized browser experiences." There is a gray area between Google Apps, extensions, and simple links to websites, but the right extensions can turn your browser into a Swiss Army knife for their usefulness and efficiency.

WHAT IS THE BENEFIT OF A TEACHER EXTENTION

You can make things easier, more accessible, more visible, more compelling, and more convenient - there are dozens of potential benefits for you in your classroom. Cut a web page with one touch on every note. Find a reference. Student model of how to add a quote. Send the link to colleagues without opening other tabs. Find a useful resource for a lesson? Shovel it. Tweet it. Pin it. Are you looking for a publication that you want to read? Don't email it to them - use Pocket.

What criteria do we use to select each extension? These extensions need to increase efficiency, improve content/courses, and you can connect with other teachers/parents/students, or improve your workflow as an educator. If you have the potential to meet one of these four criteria, it has been included.

Keep in mind that too many extensions can slow down your browser and speed is another of Chrome's talents before browsing and installing 25 of your favorites.

There is no standard for the number of extensions you should use. Your mileage may vary here. The speed of your PC, your available memory, your Wi-Fi speed, the number of open tabs and much more can affect the apparent speed of your browser. To add and remove extensions (it's as easy as a few clicks; see the video above). to optimize your settings so that Chrome remains agile and useful for you as a teacher

HIDDEN GOOGLE CLASSROOM FEATURE

In the past two years, Google Classroom has become a popular learning platform for many teachers using G Suite for Education. Through the seamless integration of G Suite tools such as Google Docs, Google Presentations, Google Sheets, Gmail, and Google Calendar, Google Classroom creates an efficient workflow for teachers and students by organizing tasks and content in an easy-to-navigate online class Site. While Google Classroom offers many great opportunities, three teachers and students, in particular, can save a lot of time and increase the efficiency of workflows. So let's use these cool features!

1 - The task plan

Google Classroom automatically creates a homework calendar to help you organize students and teachers. Whenever a teacher creates a task or question in Google Classroom and assigns a due date to it, the assignment will immediately appear in the class calendar in Google Classroom.

To find this calendar, select the three lines in the upper left corner of the screen and then select Calendar. This screen allows teachers and students to see the work assigned to the class.

Teachers will also see that the new calendar will now appear in their G Suite calendar. Calendar. In addition to adding homework to this calendar from the classroom, teachers can access it directly from the G Suite calendar to add events for the class that may not be linked to the due date. Some examples of teachers who use this calendar feature are planning school trips, planning extra tutoring time, and organizing a meeting after school. To make the calendar more accessible, you should publish it in the calendar settings and then share the URL link with the parents.

2 - The work area

Teachers and students can also use the Google Classroom workspace to collect all assignments in one place. If a teacher has not graded a particular task, it is displayed in this area. If a student has not submitted a task, it will also be displayed in their work area.

Therefore, the work area can serve as a de facto task list and help teachers and students to effectively identify and manage their workflow.

3 - Organize the class sequence with topics

A theme, a new feature in Google Classroom, allows teachers to organize the posts that they add to the "stream" in the classroom. Teachers can now assign a topic when creating an ad, task, or question. These topics act as a category for each post, so they can organize efficiently.

When a new topic is created, it will appear on the left side of the classroom stream. When a topic is selected, all posts to which that topic has been assigned are displayed. With the topic function, teachers can now organize all content in their course. For example, a history teacher could create a topic for each lesson, e.g. B. "Ancient Rome". A math teacher can create a topic for each unit or chapter he studies.

4 - Share the classroom extension

For teachers using Chrome books or laptops in their classrooms, the Chrome Share to Classroom extension enables teachers to easily view and share student work and screens for the class. With the "Share in the Classroom" extension, students can share a website on their teacher's computer. First, students click on the extension and then choose to send it to the Teacher. When this is done, the teacher will receive a pop-up notification on her screen that she must accept before the student page is displayed, as shown in the GIF below.

With the same steps, a teacher can launch a website in real-time on their students' devices!

The extension also allows teachers to create Google Classroom content directly from the extension. When a teacher finds a website that they want to post to Google Classroom as part of a task, question, or ad, they can use the extension to create one of these options.

With the "Classroom Sharing" extension, teachers and students can now easily and effectively share discoveries and stories.

While Google Classroom is known for organizing student work in Google

BEST APP FOR GOOGLE CLASSROOM

Drive, individual copies of Google Docs are made

Do you want to know which applications are connected to Google Classroom to get the best learning and teaching experience? These are the best and best apps that Google Classroom can use for better learning.

Google Classroom is essentially the future of teaching. This is a free web service developed by Google for schools, which can be easily created, distributed, and even scoring assignments on the computer, not on paper. This is also an amazing way to use less paper and save more trees! It is a great way to keep in touch with your students and stay organized in each class.

What makes Google Classroom a practical platform is a fact that there are apps you can use with it! There are apps that you can download to improve your teaching skills and allow students to learn each subject through different teaching methods. And all this is related to Google Classroom. If you already have Google Classroom and want to use other teaching tools, each of these applications that you can use with Google Classroom is for you.

While you can use this on your phone and pad, CK-12 is a very useful app with over 5,000 lessons and concepts in math, science, and spelling. You and your students can access the content anytime, anywhere. If students want to improve their grades or learn more about a subject, this application can help.

The app includes practicing and learning at your own pace, tracking progress in all subjects, working on class assignments, receiving reminders of homework deadlines, receiving recommendations for learning resources, and more. And there are so many topics this app covers, such as geometry, measurement, earth science, biology, English, spelling, money, time, calculus, chemistry, and others. Your students can understand their worst subject much better with CK-12.

Would you like you and your students to acquire knowledge every day in a very short time? Curiosity is one of the best apps for Google Classroom and it is an app that everyone can never stop learning! You can learn a lot about the world by reading articles and watching videos.

With over 5,000 articles and literally over a million videos selected, they are all based on whatever topic you can think of. You and your students can also select your favorites and mark them in the Favorites category. From history to science, this app offers countless fascinating articles and videos every day that help explain certain topics and their specific teachings.

Is teaching a language a difficult task and a difficult task for students? Duo lingo is one of the most useful apps for Google Classroom! This app works wonders and is considered the most popular app in the world for teaching and learning languages. Through the 23 languages offered from Spanish to French, Russian, Dutch, Swedish, Italian, Hebrew, and more, your students can learn to speak any language fluently with the constant practice of this application.

Duo lingo teaches a language through fun, bite-sized lessons. It can also be recorded to see what it's like to speak in a different language. As Duo the Owl tracks how you're doing, you can have real boot conversations! And yes, Duo lingo is connected to Google Classroom and one of the best applications that teachers can download.

Math and English are two of the subjects that students find difficult to understand. With IXL, students can now have fun learning through interactive questions, personalized recommendations, and virtual rewards! With over 5,700 skills in math and English, all of your students will be continually motivated and engaged as they progress topic by topic and master any new challenges that come their way.

While this app can be used from pre-K through 12th grade, all students can review lessons and practice what they have learned in the most fun way. There are many jumps in math, images for graphing square functions, and much more. English involves learning new vocabulary, reading and analyzing texts, developing writing skills, and others to improve the learning skills of your students.

WHAT IS THE APPLE CLASSROOM?

Apple Classroom is a free pad app that allows teachers to manage multiple pads in their classrooms. The teacher installs the application on their device and invites (or inserts) student iPods to become part of their class. When they join the class, the teacher's iPods inherits a collection of pseudo superpowers that they can use to monitor and manage the student learning experience

WHAT DOES THE APPLE CLASSROOM DO

The short answer may be beyond your imagination! Here is a list of the app's product descriptions in the app store.

- After the setup is complete, the "Classroom" will be connected to nearby student devices.
- The classroom intelligently assigns students to the last shared iPods they used

- At the end of a session, sign out of approved pads students to prepare for the next class
- Start, focus, or pause the student work.
- Launch an app, website or book on student devices with a tap
- Lock devices in an app so students can concentrate better
- Lock the screens to stop work or realign your class
- Mute audio on student device at the end of each lesson; review the summary of student activity and the approved inbox
- See what your students are seeing on the screen
- View an overview of all student screens at the same time
- Concentrate on a single student screen
- Students are informed when their screens are displayed
- Share documents and links with your class with Airdrop
- Share with your whole class with just a touch

- Share URLs, documents, images and more with drag & drop in iOS 11 to individual students or groups
- Students can also share with you
- Share student work in the Apple TV classroom
- Show the class the great work your students are doing
- Use airplay to wirelessly display a student's screen
- Students are informed when their screens are displayed
- Reset your managed Apple ID password without calling IT
- Organize student devices in groups.
- The classroom automatically creates groups of students based on the applications they use
- Teachers can create groups to split students into project teams.
- Carry out actions in whole groups or individual students within groups

TIPS AND TRICK FOR GOOGLE CLASSROOM

Google officially announced Google Classroom 2014. In the classroom, teachers and students can create near-perfect digital classrooms on the web. The software is tightly integrated with other Google services like Google Drive, Google Calendar, Gmail, Google Docs, and Google Forms to ensure a seamless experience. With Google Classroom, teachers can create a digital class, invite students, assign homework, ask questions, and more Google classroom.

With Google Classroom, teachers can grade assignments, communicate with students; create assignment templates and more. Now that most teachers and professors work from home, it's time to Master Google Classroom and assigns students homework to continue their studies while locked out.

In this post, we'll talk about the top eleven tips and tricks for teachers in the Google classroom. We'll start with some basics and talk about application integration and service feature sharing. Let us begin.

Visit Google Classroom

1. Change the theme and share the password

As you create a new class, you can add details like name, description, and a header image (theme template) for customization. You can choose between standard themes or upload the photo from your PC. In most cases, you will get along with the default settings as they are perfectly divided into categories like math and science, art, sports, history, and more.

Tap the selected topic in the header, select a topic, and apply it to the classroom. Copy the course code and invite students to participate in the course.

2. The color of the folder in Google Drive

This is a fairly simple option, but very important if you are working with dozens of classes and subjects at the same time. As you may already know, by default all created classes are saved in the Google Drive folder. You can change the color of the class folder for easy recognition and customization.

Go to a Class> Class work> Class Drive folder and the corresponding folder on Google Drive will open. You can rename it and add numbers to the title. Then right-click the folder to select Change Color from the context menu and assign a new folder color, which is set to dull gray by default.

3. Assignment plan

This is a must for all teachers. Google Classroom offers the ability to schedule tasks in advance. You can create assignments, add relevant details, comments, and grades, and post or schedule them for a set time. You can see the scheduled task with name and time in a gray section on the Classroom menu.

4. Use Google Calendar integration

Did you know that the Google Classroom creates a separate calendar for each class in Google Calendar? You can go to Courses> Work at home and select Google Calendar. There you will see separate calendars for the classes you have created. If you don't want your calendar to be affected, uncheck the box with your name next to it. Users can also change the color of the calendar.

5. Create reference material

As you distribute tasks, you may want to provide resource material for the project. Teachers can add titles, descriptions, and share resource files from Google Docs, Forms, YouTube, or the Web at Create> Material. Select a category and tap the "Publish" button at the top.

6. Use private comments for better communication

As you may already know, you can set overall grades for assignments. After sending students, you can give them grades. Even better, however, is that teachers can use the private comment feature to personally congratulate students.

7. Sort students by the last name and first name

When dealing with hundreds of students in the classroom, keeping track of grades can be a headache. When issuing grades, teachers can use the filter menu to sort students by the last or first name.

APPLE CLASSROOM VS GOOGLE CLASSROOM

Apple Classroom was launched in March 2016. Because of the things I read online or hear when I speak to other educators, I feel like I'm still wrong compared to Google Classroom. I can see why that happens. Both products have very similar names and were developed to solve technological problems in the classroom. However, the truth is that these two products couldn't be more different. In this post, I wanted to take some time to analyze everything Apple Classroom can do and compare it with Google Classroom to give you some ideas on how to use these useful technology tools in your school.